Curses and Wishes

Sponsored by the Academy of American Poets, the Walt Whitman Award is given annually to the winner of an open competition among American poets who have not yet published a book of poems.

JUDGE FOR 2010: MARVIN BELL

poems

Carl Adamshick

Curses and Wishes

Louisiana State University Press)|(Baton Rouge

Published by Louisiana State University Press
Copyright © 2011 by Carl Adamshick
All rights reserved
Manufactured in the United States of America
LSU Press Paperback Original
FIRST PRINTING

DESIGNER: Mandy McDonald Scallan
TYPEFACE: Whitman
PRINTER AND BINDER: IBT Global

Grateful acknowledgment is made to the editors of the following publications, in which the poems listed
first appeared: *American Literary Review*, "Iphigenia," "Night," "War as the cherry blossoms"; *American
Poet*, "Benevolence," "Our flag"; *American Poetry Review*, "Out past the dead end sign"; *Harvard Review*,
"Harvard, Illinois"; *Mid-American Review*, "The confession of an apricot," "Dissection," "Nurs-
ing," "The emptiness"; *The Oregonian*, "Home"; *PoetLore*, "The book of Nelly Sachs." "Oyster bar" first
appeared in "Oyster Suite," a limited-edition portfolio published by Charles Seluzicki in 2010.

Library of Congress Cataloging-in-Publication Data

Adamshick, Carl, 1969–
  Curses and wishes : poems / Carl Adamshick.
    p. cm.
  ISBN 978-0-8071-3776-5 (pbk. : alk. paper)
  I. Title.
  PS3601.D399C87 2011
  811'.6—dc22

2010029103

4824 2134
4/12

Contents

Curses and Wishes

Even though

Even though you regretted sleeping
with him, you didn't regret sleeping with him.

Even though you loved him, you didn't love him.

You were trying, even though you knew you weren't trying.

You could see another world in this world,
even though you knew

there was only one world.

The street is doing that thing to the moon I like.
Birds have taken their paths through the trees.

May happiness be a wheel, a lit throne, spinning
in the vast pinprick of darkness.

We forget almost everything,
even though we believe we live to remember.

Oblivion and significance
brush our bones, leave us weeping for strangers.

May your secrets remain hidden
in that beautiful place covered in suffering.

I see loneliness
as a shell of mottled smoke in a high nest
of metal shavings, a cold

autumn day without wind, the sun unfolding
an ancient map on parched ground
we can't read, even though

our language comes from the earth.

I felt the deep bruise of a sentence
and wanted to eat
at the banquet of silence.

May betrayal be a way home;

the coming back, a burden of joy.
A general un-understanding has left me
both open and closed, overwhelmed
by the magnitude of the world's choices,

but also, at ease,
floating on the light wave of its being.

May the defilement of hope be a coronation.
May you wear the crown of exile.

May you forget what you hold dear.

Life is and cannot be
a failure.

Hatred sleeps in the white blooming
lilac branch of the skull.

I live in my mother's maiden name.
I was taken in as an ocean
takes in daylight.

Mourn, if you must mourn,
feel loss as the only profound thing we share,

even though you believe
each of us is alone forever in an endless field
of carbon.

May the dice have no eyes
and may you keep throwing them on the table's
green velvet.

May you have night,
with its dark branches, every night.

Memoir

I feel something impossibly small
that might become pain

as I slide a piece of paper
under everything
my mother has said.

New year's morning

A low, quiet music is playing—
distorted trumpet, torn bass line,
white windows. My palms
are two speakers the size
of pool-hall coasters.
I lay them on the dark table
for you to repair.

Harvard, Illinois

When someone moved to town,
we went mad wondering what caused it.
A whole family
come to settle in the green house
two doors down from the end.
The grain elevator
blocking the sun from three on.
If he was going to work the fields
or on cars. If her hair
was the only toy the children had.

Junkyard

I never visit my younger self.
Any change I elicit
would be just that: change.
Something different in a world
of differences. A shifting
from memory to dream. Snow
falling in a barrel of rusted
engine parts becoming a day
of lightning and old fallen oak:
one life or another, mine or yours.
This is the last outpost before
things become what they are.
I was eleven when an older self,
the lord of my childhood, appeared
above the chair in my room
splendid and silent like a planet
rotating, spinning in its ellipses,
but, also, unmoving by the headboard
and the one pillow full of feathers.

Compassion

It could have been a whale's heart
she towed in her wagon.

It looked like an ocean sponge
with a red viscous beating.

We watched,
not knowing
how she managed.

It was sad and strange
how her heart had become her burden.

Home

You had been gone a few days.
The place went looking for you,

unaware you were returning.

I remained lonely in the evening
when the moon broadcasted

silence through the dust.

My love was once
a faint blue tear
of thin glass glowing
in my chest.

Now my love is you.

It must be three in the afternoon
and I am trying to sleep
on your side of the bed.

Our flag

should be green
to represent an ocean.
It should have two stars
in the first canton,
for us and navigation.
They should be of gold thread,
placed diagonally,
and not solid,
but comprised of lines.
Our flag should be silky jet.
It should have a wound,
a red river the sun must ford
when flown at half-mast.
It should have the first letter
of every alphabet ever.
When folded into a triangle
an embroidered eighth note
should rest on top
or an odd-pinnate,
with an argentine stem,
a fiery leaf, a small branch
signifying the impossible song.
Or maybe honey and blue
with a centered white pinion.
Our flag should be a veil
that makes the night weep
when it comes to dance,
a birthday present we open
upon death, the abyss we sleep
under. Our flag should hold
failure like light glinting
in a headdress of water.
It should hold the moon
as the severed head

of a white animal
and we should carry it
to hospitals and funerals,
to police stations and law offices.
It should live, divided,
deepening its yellows
and reds, flaunting itself
in a dead gray afternoon sky.
Our flag should be seen
at weddings well after
we've departed.
It should stir in the heat
above the tables and music.
It should watch our friends
join and separate
and laugh as they go out
under the clouded night
for cold air and cigarettes.
Our flag should sing
when we cannot,
praise when we cannot,
rejoice when we cannot.
Let it be a reminder.
Let it be the aperture,
the net, the rope of dark stars.
Let it be mathematics.
Let it be the eloquence
of the process shining
on the page, a beacon
on the edge of a continent.
Let its warnings be dismissed.
Let it be insignificant
and let its insignificance shine.

Dissection

We wanted to save
the dead animals.

We took a skinned
cat being refrigerated
in a clear bag.

Outside dark
and shadow talked
on the kept grass.

We could think of nothing.

We tore a hole
in the thick plastic,

raised the glistening
creature up the flagpole.

Nursing

It has become clear
the woman in the warehouse
is being beaten.

I think of Illinois,
its endless horizon,
and how, evenings
when I couldn't
sleep, I would hear
a 'possum come feed
on the pig's teat.

Hope

I thought of a day—
just one
when we all lived perfectly.
I thought
of what that would do for us,
how we would celebrate
the anniversary of perfection.
I dreamed so long
I burned up
on re-entry.

Benevolence

We took your food and in a few days
you'll see we took your excrement.

We've devised such intricate rules.

We've agreed, signed papers. We took the papers.

We took your pain, your dignity.
We took your language and watched
as religion fell from you.

We took your death,
strung it as a jewel on a silver chain
and showed it to you
as just another thing you don't have.

Iphigenia

War never starts with blood.

It takes something smaller,
a radio sounding of tall grass.

A horse pulling wood on the shore

is a figure of her.
The day is all pain and glory

stuffed in night's belly. The brothers

believe her blood will fill sails.
They are nothing without wind.

They are weak, small, their ganglia hot.

One says: the importance of the feast is death.
One says: take her clothes off so it's real.

They didn't know they couldn't kill me.

The knife opened a deer's neck,
snapped and severed its shuddering cords.

All history comes to rest

in words
that appeal to your aesthetics

or don't. Like the mind

or the dead feasting,
with and on itself,

the further within the word you go,

you only find
more word, more mind, more dead.

Arithmetic

The last note left the clarinet and couldn't

rise

in the heavy morning fog.
It stayed close

to the musician
who watched it change, then drop
as a dark gray bead.

None of the notes rose. They lay on the grass.
Some on top of others
and broken.
Primo Levi

go and be counted   go and be

where the blood ceases.
Go   be with your family and leave

the university of memory.

The book of Nelly Sachs

The field of her tongue
described ash in the treeline.

Her spine, stitched through the countryside,
carried the living freight.
The dead

found relief in the hollow mass of her lungs.

You may not know this,
but when you talk about the night
and its stars

you talk about her
sacrifice at the wall of alphabets

and how, when she chose
to spell the sorrow of a holocaust,

she lost her body.

Sleep

Night comes to read you again.

On page eight thousand forty-eight
a paragraph ends:

The quiet birds tend the quiet birds.

Night closes you gently,
leans against the train window,
begins to think of its motherland.

War as the cherry blossoms

We turn and turn and turn the soil of ourselves.

We prepare the same ancient armature.
The deception of language

is that we are beautiful, that we give and care

as the cherry blossoms
fall in the high heat of noon.

To think each moment
is new, that we are constantly beginning,
and what we do is what we have always done:

bury the dead in the vault of earth.

It's a disgrace.
We watch the season as it lets everything

rise and open.

Branches full of green. Our memory
that chain
we feel every time we walk.

The emptiness

I didn't want to give my body to war.
I saw news footage of a fly

in a dead man's mouth. I saw a man
made to kneel and then told,

in a language he couldn't
comprehend, to lie flat on his stomach.

The camera caught the bullets entering
his spine, the base of his skull

and then the men walked away
          from the emptiness.

The camera, too, turned and ran
through leaves, green and lashing.

If it had stayed, we would have seen rain
pelt the soldier's back, wash his fatigues.

We would have seen his body as insects
lived on the continent of his flesh,

lived until he was bone, until he was dirt,
          until his emptiness sang.

I was afraid of the men walking,
of seeing the sky, lightly clouded, as blood

flowed out of my body. I dreamt
of a helmet with a butchered foot beside it

and knew it was my brother's,
but couldn't remember his name.

I left the green grass of high school,
walked under the tall oaks

to the post office.
I filled in the little boxes with the letters

of my name,
looked out the plate-glass window

at a four-way stop, a flag limp in the heat,
in the bright air. I signed,

telling them where I lived,
that I was willing, that when they sent

the card I'd wear the uniform.
But I lied. I couldn't

have been fitted for the infantry garb,
the sanguinary rank.

In the weeks that followed
I felt occupied, silenced like a clean,

smooth conch echoing the sea,
an open urn.

                The emptiness of my mouth
began. I wanted to say I'd seen

the tree of night,
its crown holding the great stars,

the beginning recorded in the center
ring of its bole,

but said nothing.
I saw that we were the ancient text,

the blood, the next inscription
on the unending trunk,

and said nothing.
I stood there and in seeing its splendor

was injured
by the senselessness of my nights and days.

The forked branch of my existence
was lit like a crack

of lightning.
My breath, my tongue, the broken font

of my voice had wanted to praise.
And when I didn't speak

I became a secret, a testimony
against my own body. I lived and lived

with the fact that I watched others
struggle and pray.

I watched them lie on the shore
with their heads adrift in a shine of stars

and wanted their hunger
to finally consume their sad, hurting bodies.

I watched, hoping
when the tide came and lifted them away

I could live without shame.
                    The emptiness. The tongue bound

to the betrayal
held in the mouth, to the apology held

in the mouth, to the brutal remains
held in the socket of the mouth.

And still, under it all,
I feel an orchid, the cold river flow

around my feet. I see the stars
as the shimmering bones

of migratory birds
and swallow the humiliating taste

of beauty. I am the dirt,
the worm-dirge, the lament and procession

winding through a garden burning
with flowers.

I am not the body that dies naked,
swollen and torn,

infested with beetles.
I am not the body that lacks

its funeral and its offering of plums.
I am not the body,

              the empty midnight station.
I am not the bombed-out factory,

its machinery covered in snow.
I am veins and breath, the entrance

and exit the world passes through.
I see a quickening end in a blue,

twisted cord and know I am its habitation.
I see the severed hands of a war

and feel it
escape into me like a tired lover

I comfort into the dark hours,
where my body, swathed with heat

and sorrow, listens to air
pass through the gate of its teeth.

The wonderment of being
in the hive, in the astonishment of days,

when light around the field is spilt moon
and memory is a nest

of mud and grass hidden in the bright
summer branches,

              when emptiness is an open door,
the well-black pupil of an iris.

I am lost in the living, in the acceptance
of rain filling a bucket,

in the belief
that the chemical burn was a washing

for the exodus
and the smoke rising through the chimneys

into the pale blue morning was a love song.
There are days when I wake

and find my face is a hole
and I have nowhere to hang my mask.

Correction

Last week the caption
on page twelve stated
the person photographed
was Jerzy Lem when in fact
it was Adolf Hitler.

Night

Maybe you want to forget
what the world has shown you.
Maybe you want to lie down
in the quiet. A somber wave
breaks over you at the end
of the movie when the house
lights come up. Your friend
is a suicide. Somewhere
far from you a lake turns
from a dark cold-green
into a sheet of ink.
You feel if it came close
and asked, you would give
the world whatever it needed.

The confession of an apricot

I love incorrectly.

There is a solemnity in hands,
the way a palm will curve in
accordance to a contour of skin,
the way it will release a story.

This should be the pilgrimage.
The touching of a source.
This is what sanctifies.

This pleading. This mercy.
I want to be a pilgrim to everyone,
close to the inaccuracies, the astringent
dislikes, the wayward peace, the private
words. I want to be close to the telling.
I want to feel everyone whisper.

After the blossoming I hang.
The encyclical that has come
through the branches
instructs us to root, to become
the design encapsulated within.

Flesh helping stone turn tree.

I do not want to hold life
at my extremities, see it prepare
itself for my own perpetuation.
I want to touch and be touched
by things similar in this world.

I want to know a few secular days
of perfection. Late in this one great season
the diffused morning light
hides the horizon of sea. Everything
the color of slate, a soft tablet
to press a philosophy to.

The farm

The broken stile is covered in leaves.
Once I sat there and felt
I was the snow
holding the family's footprints.

Oyster bar

Gone are the knives
and the wet newspapers,
the split shells,
their raw, cold moisture,

the ocean quietly
laying its salt down
beyond the window.

I hope the room
leading into death
has these lamps,

that our farewell
to everything
has this ease
and lasts as long as us
ordering another ale
to wait out the rain.

Pelican

We walked in a light gray light
on the shore of the Pacific
where we could see farther north
a molten hue gouging out a break
in the cloudbank. I remember it being cold
but being dressed for cold.

She was saying she and her mother picked blackberries
in a morning fog the day she moved away,
that her parents were still alive
and it had been a day of small errands.

I told her I had never been to a funeral.

My cousin explained the ice
as a thin transparent mold growing
on the face he found half buried in snow.

We came to a grassy area with benches.

Within memory there is no sound
and really there is no image.

Night is space and snow
something enormous, broken and falling.

You join the sad parade
when you are alone thinking
of what you don't want to be thinking of.

A disturbing display of myself
follows a quiet marching band, my float,
covered in white gardenias,
the moon, asleep on my lap.

My bones have been pulled out,
made into the chair I sit on.
I wave to the invisible crowd,
glide under their wreaths and lanterns.

The joy leaving me was so beautiful
it brought me joy in its going.

That evening ducks were picking shards
of bread left in the deep grass.

A pelican scooped one of the ducks
into its pouch.

We were young in the gray-darkening light.
The hole in the sky was a red-amplified
music of light thumping at a decibel beyond reason.

Fluency

I clear the chessboard of pieces

and find religion
is a word, that governments are words.

I find meaning
only when the letters are left undisturbed.

The board could be an acre of timothy
or a ballroom
waiting to be scuffed by shined shoes.

I find my mother
curled in the shell of tradition, the gilded triangles

at her breast bone. I find her lost,

dreaming of light—a child
unaware the promise was made to keep her quiet.

And then, of course, I could make her faith

a white inflorescence,
a trumpet and vine pattern on a pleated summer dress.
I could give it the grace of cloth.

That is why I fear the uses of language
and love
that comes and undresses itself

like an autumn tree. I see her suffering

because she trusted. I see her staring at her arms,
astonished at how loss
can have the same weight as an infant.

Almost

The rain is almost
falling
like snow.

Some three a.m. car passes.

The corner utility pole
holds a cone of light
to its mouth

and is screaming
at the pavement.

We are almost here
suffering,
almost drifting through

the world without purpose

as the rain vanishes
in the darkness
beyond.

Out past the dead end sign

There! Look me full in the face!—in the face. Understand, if you can,
That the eyes of such women as I am are clean as the palm of a man.
—ELIZABETH BARRETT BROWNING

Last night, touching the skin
that has become your eyes,
I fell into a charred landscape
I recognized from childhood.
Once green. I touched,
once and once, the fastened
lids of your face. Forgive me,
for what I think, for what
I sometimes believe I want.

And

A year into our marriage I lost my eyes.
They were blowfish pulled from the sea,
two balled-up, quivering hedgehogs,
dead rats, Victorian paperweights.
Wet and swollen, they fell from my face.
My muddy grenades, my receipts,
my teacups of warm rain. Amnions.
I carried one in each hand, weeping.

And

We make our own pain.
I was once dumb enough
to believe this. I remember

making the box, dovetailed
cherry, burning into the wood
my devotion. I only wanted
your grief, wanted to watch
it drift toward the center
of a small lake and sink
where the moon struck water.
But you never get just one
thing and you never know
how what you get might
flourish like something
delicate under hothouse
glass. Your eyes are in
the lake of my body. I quiet
every time they turn and focus
on a different aspect
of the still black. I thought
the offering would allow
them sleep, free your hands
from their weeping, but,
it has become our argument.
The angry staves humming
for want in our one sad duet.

And

My husband's body is soft.
I touch him in the dark.
I have darkness like death.
I see the way his stomach
sees: churning blood;
a whiteness of black
racing toward a pinpoint;

an infinite conical field.
I hear a sitcom open loud
in the living room.
I could hate him
like other women hate
their husbands. Their pleasure
one of secrecy and small.
They must love their own
commitment; sycophants
giving themselves
to the fervent hands,
to the risen penis,
letting that dark room shield
them from the warm,
bright sperm, which in the end,
it doesn't do. That dark
ties them to the invisible,
glorious bleeding. It's not hate
I feel. It's something deeper
moving in something darker,
more significant. It has nothing
to do with him or me
or television. It's unconcerned
with our lives. I love my husband
as I love life in all its confusions
and joys. When I take him
in my hands, I know the buses
stop running. Still, when I lead
him to the bed and my mouth
opens on his open mouth,
I know the world closes in
to listen and waits for us to return.

And

I can't help but think you gave them away,
left them on a park bench for that child
to find. Green, light as fresh marjoram.
When they were shrouded in your skin,
when they lived in your body, I studied
them as a brewer marveling fermentation.
The heart knows nothing. It just moves
its blood, chamber to chamber. They
glossed over in sex. Focused on something
beyond the room, their watery curves, loose
as muscles in a milk bath, would whisper
the names of currents, stars, jasper and jade,
whatever I was thinking. I wanted to live
in them, lonely, listening to the music
you couldn't hear from the outside.

And

When you weren't home I would put my finger
in the rut of your devotion.

And

I'd like to say something
about drinking. *Cleansed.*
My friend from high school
would say after vomiting.
He would drink that much,
always. In winter, in the back
of a school bus, its green
seats edged with dirty white

vinyl, we would sip from
the same bottle. The moon,
exceedingly bright. The snow
lit like fluorescence. We never
left anything behind. I think
that's how it is. No one
suspects if you're careful.
Years now, I've talked
to myself. Once, I convinced
myself to stay. Some days
her anger is an encompassing
silence, radiating. You
have to walk through it
like a stagnant night in August.
You let that slide.
You let most things slide.
You yearn for friction,
anything; a funeral, just
so you can touch the flowers.
I don't know what happened
to my friend. Maybe habit
got the best of him. A few
times, we woke on the flat
graveled roof of the school;
the sun low on the plains.
Our heads awful, pained
with the prospect of climbing
down and entering, again,
the town where we lived.
I know lives have more
than one love. We curl
toward one another
in the night without certainty;
drift in our own waiting,
shimmer like taillights

on the rise of a wet road
before setting into the black
horizon. Here, in an hour past
midnight, I dream of holding
you as I'm holding you.

And

I invented him
a lover, then a grass widow.
Their engagements
in a third-floor studio;
a light watery blue shell of a room.
His lips, like cloud-shadow,
floating over her back as he talked
about his difficult love with me.

And

When my brother brought home *Nebraska*
the needle, blind in the black groove,
scraped out a song. That night,
I put on the headphones and listened
as my family slept. I knew I was going
to move. I knew this song the needle
revolved in was my life. I knew the needle
blind in the song sang. I saw the wind
enter the corn to lie down like so many
waitresses and assembly line workers
coming home to sleep after a double.

And

I saw light as a sanctuary.
I thought a shadow meant a body,
that there were things
you couldn't refute,
like ice melting in the palm.
The box was missing
for a week, before the boy
opened it and showed me
his plane and fire truck.

And

I'm thinking of friends
who have left marriages
in the same fashion
they entered them:
like dreamy teenagers,
or like a glass of wine, half-finished,
at a table where the diners
were too sated to finish.

And

Everything is a wall underground
until that stranger opens my eyes.
Twenty, maybe, a soft thumb
of flesh in the crotch of his legs.

All I can hear is my husband,
feel him trying to help.
She makes a fist around his flesh,
moves it in that light your eyes grow
accustomed to in bed. They kiss.
He's trying to peel her underwear
down. Divorced from dreams,
we have become our bodies.
And that young couple showing
me how they love is what I have:
a nipple, a finger, an earlobe,
a memory, the whole day
descending like a red carpet.
His navel full of semen.

He puts salted butter on the table
and returns to the kitchen
for the plate of radish.
She turns a rind of lemon
into her water. We wait
long enough to hear them talk
about night, long enough
to hear them say if you keep
digging through that darkness
you strike a vein of starlight,
long enough for them to clean
the dishes, turn off the lights,
close the curtains, long enough
to see them move around
each other in the bathroom,
long enough only to hear him
explaining the trestle
and how the two huge engines
in the late afternoon dark

shone in the falling wetness
just a few feet above the rising river.

And

Three in the morning,
I went out in the car,
out past the milk factory
where the road T-bones,
out past the dead end sign
on Hillcrest. I got out,
wedged myself between
the barbed wire and walked
among the cattle. I wanted
a burden I could love,
a life of enormity and there,
in that field, I held everything;
all my memories of this bankrupt town.
The public pool where we climbed
the fence and drank silo cans
until dawn, the house where I first
shed my clothes before a stranger
and smoked cigarettes with her
in the attic, the porch swing still there
hanging in the light, the train yard.
I remembered the accidents, the girl
who lost her leg to a riding mower,
the cousin of my brother's friend
who hit that cemetery oak
early one November morning
in his new red car, the stories of him,
passed out, slumped over the wheel
with the passenger's door open

in front of the Hendersons' house.
The way he tore out of there, they say,
to let them know. And my first job,
at sixteen, having to confront the owner
of the restaurant about what he owed me;
his office just a desk in the basement.
The pregnant woman who worked there,
and would ask me to come over
to watch movies because her husband
was out. I realized she was only
three years older than me, finally
understanding the sadness
of her asking. I was immense
and empty out there. I filled myself
with their lives, I stored up
the whole town, generations
of the town, other towns.
I have them now and it's nothing.
When I came to the edge of the field,
the sun was just beginning to press
through the mesh of darkness.
I had walked miles, had miles to walk.
Do you understand what I am saying?
I came home, to these rooms,
to this place, to you. This is it.
These are the days. Know
that your mouth and heart
will be twisted through with root
and worm. Know that you cannot
change what has happened,
that it can only distance itself from you,
grow weak, that humiliation and regret
die like everything, that we go on
from here like we have always gone on.
Everything changes like the seasons.

It's summer, but it's not last summer.
Do not live so close to me and unhappy.
What has happened is not my fault.
If you want to live preparing a defense,
if you want to live blaming,
if you want to merely dream about floating
in the Aegean at dusk, do it without me.
Here. Here is where we begin again,
change, find ourselves chest-deep kissing
in the wet moon. Here, now, we need
to silence all this waiting.

And

Before the martini
spilled into the stereo
causing an electrical short
that almost closed
the evening down early
and before you put
your head under my dress
on the dance floor,
and before your brother
puked on my mother's shoes,
we cut the cake and watched
our friends eat and slip
from their formalities.
Before the rings, your father's
loud snuffling, his wet hankie,
before the drive to church
when my mother said
she was so glad I was finally
marrying, before working

my way into the dress,
and before the breakfast
of melon and toast,
we slept in a hotel,
we sat on the bed joking
of what might go wrong,
speculating on who would
say what to who, how we
laughed, readying ourselves
for the show. We knew.
We lived right where we knew,
so comfortably. You know
I'd take you talking
to my mother civilly,
with decency and love,
before I took the Aegean.
I'd take a late afternoon
in bed slowly turning
to an evening of old movies
and popcorn, not the Aegean.
I'd take another reception
of drunken mistakes,
not the Aegean.
I'd take holidays without
the gripes about my sister.
I'd take sex with more talk.
I'd take your tongue
and penis without the past.
I'd take two flowers
you picked and put
in a clean beer bottle,
not the Aegean.
I'd take made beds.
I'd take the front stoop
and the neighbor's tree

all fucking green
in the warm dusk
before I'd take the Aegean.
I'm not the dreamy one.
I know exactly where we live.
I know what I take.
I take you always, shaky
and uncertain, remembering
things too fondly through
nostalgia's veil. And your
dreams are of the same tulle.
I don't think about the Aegean
or new beginnings.
That's you, living
between your two veils.
There is no end,
except the end. I know you
pity me, tire of always having
to drive, always having
to pick the cans and packages
off the grocery shelves,
not believing me
when I tell you the box
is open and a man
and a woman are in a dark
hallway, their backs bare.
The red light growing
smaller near the end.

Acknowledgments

I'd like to thank the following people in the following ways. This book would never have happened without them. My gratitude is endless and my appreciation lies down beside it.

For the books:
Charles Seluzicki

For the writing:
Matthew Dickman, Michael Dickman, Michael McGriff,
Joseph Millar, Dorianne Laux

For the pen and the paper and the love:
Jessie Hibbs